Finding the Ultimate Purpose to Life

Greg Crawford

Published by:

Creative Release Publishing

Des Moines, Iowa

thebaseiowa.org

Printed in the United States

First printing 2009

ISBN – 13: 978-1481218313

Table of Contents

Introduction

Introduction

Because I have ministered to so many people in the Body of Christ and witnessed their struggles with many issues, I went on a quest to find some ultimate solutions to settle the very essence of who they really are. This book is the combination of a teaching series and revelations the Lord has given to me to do just that. This is not just a book that has been written as a concept but the teaching inside its covers are proven and have produced fruitfulness, before going into print.

The one thing that seems to hinder us more than anything is the question "who am I"? People tell us who we are to be. Parents have told us 'this is who you are'. But the individuality of a person knows there is someone greater inside. The second common question is "what will I do with my life that will really count?" The world tells us who we are and what is expected of us, thus putting unrealistic expectations and a feeling of failure if we do not perform. God has always told people who they are first and then what they will do.

The identity of the Church today and its leaders is very unsettled and we see this being reflected in the Church not functioning in the great dynamic we all dream of. Since we function out of identity, our expressions and how we approach things is very lacking. I have endeavored to show how to find identity, purpose and to finish your life in destiny.

This book is focused more on young adults as they have their whole life ahead to be productive if these great truths are applied. However, it is also for the older generation to finally settle the issues that perhaps have plagued their understanding their whole life. I trust your concepts and thinking about yourself will now be seen how God sees you and His plan for your life. It is never too late to change the course into your ultimate destiny and future!

Chapter 1

Wandering Aimlessly

Change is always occurring in our world. In our fast paced society, it is a challenge just to stay on top of things. With computers, play stations and other electronic gear advancing so rapidly, geared towards our young adults, so does society as well. It is hard to deal with all the decisions that need to be made in a day's time, let alone in planning out the rest of your life.

It is a time for many young adults to ask, "Just how do I fit into this society? What exactly is my place and how do I get there?" These two questions seem to plague the minds and actions of every young person stretching into adulthood. Without solid answers, some will waste their lives on things that have no bearing and little satisfaction and impact.

The generation that is now on the face of the earth has the greatest advantage of any previous one to make an impact with their lives. Education, technology, and opportunity all seem to be at hand. One other ingredient is also present; a dream in young people's hearts that says their life will make a difference. But the question remains, why so many suicides, teen pregnancies, and drug addictions with young people today?

Some lack relationships with their parents and families and are looking for love and acceptance in other areas. Some have lost hope of the dream in their heart ever coming to pass and depression and despair settle in. Still others are trying to fill a void by being so different that others will notice them. But all these things come to bear in one area, a lack of true understanding of "why" they exist. Without purpose, people let everything around them erode away at their lives, until nothing seems to remain.

The question that I have to ask you is two fold. What would you do if you had no fear? No fear of people, circumstances, or of being rejected. Fear drives us many times in our lives. Fear leads us to make wrong choices. Fear also stops us from finding the dream in our heart and seeing we have purpose in life. God wants you to have confidence in who you are and the reason that your life exists. Imagine living each day not worrying about your future, but walking in confidence of the next steps you are about to take.

The second question is: how sure are you about your destiny? Without a sure understanding of our future, we end up aimlessly wandering trying to grope in the dark in the hope we will find what we will do with our life. Not being sure of the future also opens the door for fear. The uncertainty of life, and making right choices can grip our hearts at times and almost freeze us from making any decision or taking any action. We just join the rest of the crowd and try to blend in. How certain are you the rest of the crowd is right? Aren't you an individual? Do you realize every person on the earth was uniquely created with a specific task and reason for existence? When we follow others instead of trying to discover our own purpose and destiny for ourselves, we allow them to define who we are. We put ourselves into the mold of what others expect and not what we really desire.

This generation is created to be history changers and a history making generation. What if I told you the answer to make this a reality in your life? What if you could answer the question that you have no fear and that you are sure of where you are going with your life? Would you be interested enough to find out, or are you going to continue on the same path as others and not really go anywhere with your life?

This booklet is to help you see things from a different perspective, a higher perspective than you have ever seen before. Instead of getting advice from peers or even adults, why not get advice from the one who created everyone, God Himself. I am not talking about abstract religious structures that have no meaning and are full of pompous ceremony. I am talking about truly knowing how God Himself thinks about you for who you are as He made <u>you</u>, unique, special, and full of purpose. All I ask is for an open mind and that you give God twenty minutes of your time and read the pages that follow.

Change is coming to the Church, to affect the world, as God calls us from passivity to pursuit. Israel wandered for 40 years trying to find their destiny. Between the Old and New Testaments, the people of God wandered for 400 years. Many wandered and yet others found their destiny. What made the difference between the two? The answer lies in the Word of

God. This study will bring a new revelation to the destiny and purpose God has for every human being.

We can never advance or see the Kingdom of God in the earth without having a pursuit mentality. As the people of Israel left the wilderness and prepared for their destiny to unfold, they had to be repositioned first. **(Joshua 3:1-7)** Right now, the Church is positioned at the banks of the Jordan, not in the wilderness. At the Jordan, Israel received instruction concerning the destiny and purpose before them. You, too, are at this very point, with your greatest future before you. Your decisions will always affect your destiny.

Israel had to change their mentality from being survivors and followers to being pursuers and leaders. We are a generation born in the wilderness and never trained for pursuit, because we have never had a clear understanding of our future. What must we pursue to radically change our future? Two elementary things:

   1. We must pursue God's purposes for the earth.

2. We must pursue our future in those purposes.

Our lives were created and put into the earth for a plan that only God has the full knowledge. As we pursue His plan for the earth, we see how we fit into that place of effectiveness. Whether it is working a job, raising a family, or doing some radical thing, it all is connected in some way with the overall plan of God unfolding in the earth. As we pursue and understand God's plan, we see our purpose as well.

The realization of our pursuit will be released by properly positioning ourselves before Him. The place of repositioning is the place where the Spirit of God is flowing, the Jordan. Many things occurred at this place of "crossing over" to the other side and into our destiny. Our destiny is where God is. It is in the very heart of God, locked up with His hands upon it, until we pursue enough for Him to release it into our hands to walk it out.

We will never attain our destiny if we stay in a place that had blessing at one time, either. Our future is always unfolding before us, not in our yesterday or our past. Too many times, I have seen a large call or destiny upon people with a reluctance to relocate, change churches, or be involved with people who could help unlock their destiny. Others may be content to stay where they are, saying "I am in a comfortable place". They are without opposition, desiring to breakout, but without confidence of their destiny, frozen in fear of the future.

Many today continue to wander aimlessly, yet their destiny is always present and even calling to them. Their reluctance to move into the future holds a grip on their lives. Israel carried the memory of blessing with them, but not the actual blessing of fresh manna, when they crossed over into destiny. What they did carry with them is what we all carry into destiny, and that is the presence of the Lord and His hope of destiny in us. May we all be more concerned about the Kingdom mandate upon our lives than the past or even the present blessing.

The same pattern holds true in the book of *Acts Chapters 1 & 2*. Jesus called them and had spoken destiny over their lives of being witnesses after the power of God came upon them. They had to decide to move from being spectators to being participators who would accomplish destiny and purpose. This decision enabled them to cross over their Jordan in the upper room and enter into destiny upon the streets of Jerusalem. Their lives were radically changed as they entered a new life in the Spirit, life that contained purpose. They went from wandering to becoming a sign and a wonder.

There are two areas where destiny is released into our lives: individually and corporately. In the Old Testament, the prophetic was the main focus and individual destiny fulfilled changed the course of nations. In the New Testament, apostolic government became the main focus and brought change to a group of individuals who corporately found their destiny and affected the world. This requires individual destiny fitting within the confines of the corporate. We see this in *Acts 2:32-37, 41-47*. Today, individual destiny never finds fulfillment outside of the corporate destiny of God! Our lives are connected to the large overall plan of God.

As we pursue the promises of God, we are actually pursuing the individual roadmap that He has prepared for us. Every promise from the Word of God and every prophecy received is God Himself giving us direction and revealing His plan toward us.

The main area we need to pursue is the Kingdom of God and His purposes within that Kingdom. We are all part of His Kingdom whether we participate or not in any religious activity. Jesus is still your Lord even if you do not acknowledge Him. He is the One in charge of this spiritual Kingdom. In that Kingdom, you were born to have a part of its unfolding, hence your destiny!

When we begin to see through Kingdom eyes, we begin to see the ultimate purposes and plans of God and how we fit into these plans. As we do this, we begin to see the enemies of God in different dimensions, and we also begin to rise up and pursue them. We begin to take charge of our own lives in Christ. We realize things are not just going to happen and suddenly we will find our destiny. We have to realize God is partnering with us in our destiny and He expects us to take steps of faith toward it.

This will bring us to the greatest pursuit of our lives and that is not only towards our destiny but also to God Himself. You see, the destiny of every man, woman and child is found in the very heart of God. To pursue Him and what is in His heart is to pursue our destiny without really knowing it. Once we get a revelation of God's great love, concern and willingness for us to understand our reason for existence, we also begin to see that every son and daughter has a destiny their Father desires for them to attain.

Sons and daughters are the only ones who inherit the provision from the Father to fulfill destiny. *Malachi 4:6, Romans 8:14-17*. We are all sons and daughters of the King who desires for us to fully know our destiny and purpose! We must pursue His presence before we pursue His purpose. Church, it is time to pass over, cross over, and pursue our future in Him!

We must keep our eyes on the Ark (presence of God) and go after it. The Ark and worship will lead us into a new way. Since we have not passed this way before, we dare not miss its course! His presence is already in front of us. As we step forward in faith, we step into the place God's presence has already been and His purposes for us have been deposited in advance. As we pursue God, we are stepping into His footsteps. He has removed hindrances out of our pathway. He has deposited things needed for fulfillment in our lives. He has already marked the trail of life for us so we cannot fail.

Part of the corporate destiny is realizing that one person's destiny unlocks another person's destiny. We see this Biblical pattern in the Scriptures. Parts of the corporate destiny are the leaders God has appointed over your life. They can help release your destiny by having vision and speaking into your life.

Many today do not respond to their leaders in proper ways and thus delay their destiny. The Word of the Lord to the churches in Revelation (Chapters 2 and 3) was directed through each church's leadership. The saints in these churches could hear the Lord, but it was their leadership that received the word for corporate correction and for the corporate strategy needed in each city where they were located. In Acts, we see leadership directing the corporate and thus releasing the individual destiny of multitudes.

We need to follow anointed Godly leaders and not peers. Godly leaders must give an account before God of your life and how they helped you find your purpose. Peers do not have to give an account for you. This responsibility on leaders is more than helping you answer spiritual questions. It is to help you in all areas of life, since everything in our lives is intertwined, it does have a bearing upon other areas. Everything in our lives creates who we are.

Chapter 2

God's Thoughts and Intentions Toward Us

When we say we desire to know our destiny, we actually desire to know God's thoughts and intentions toward us. ***Proverbs 29:18*** *Where there is no vision, the people perish: but he that keepeth the law, happy is he.*

Vision = divine communication. Root word: to behold – see

Perish = refuse, let go, lose restraint

God reveals this divine communication through His Word. Our destiny seems hidden to us but is found in the very heart of God towards us. ***Jeremiah 1:5*** *Before I formed thee in the belly I knew thee; and before thou camest forth out of the womb I sanctified thee, and I ordained thee a prophet unto the nations.*

Formed = fashioned by divine activity

Knew = recognize you, considered you, to make one's

13

self known. It means far more than intellectual knowledge. It was used to describe the intimate relations experienced by a husband and wife.

Sanctified = dedicated, separated, treated as sacred

Ordained = give, to set, granted, trusted

Jeremiah's destiny was already planned. Esther's destiny was also already planned. (Esther, you have entered into the kingdom for such a time as this). God has a specific plan and purpose for every individual's life before they are even created. This plan is not just something we will do but a state of intimacy God has toward us. He knows everything about us.

Ephesians 2:10 For we are his workmanship, created in Christ Jesus unto good works, which God hath before ordained that we should walk in them.

Workmanship = that which is made, **work of art or masterpiece**

Hath before ordained = to prepare before, to make ready beforehand

Walk = to make one's way, progress, to make due use of opportunities. To live, to regulate one's life, to conduct one's self, to pass one's life.

We are a workmanship, a masterpiece, prepared in advance, not while we were still in our mother's womb, but before we were created in the womb. God's thoughts toward us before the womb dictated what workmanship He would create. He makes no mistakes. He sees and values each person. This is why His Son, Jesus, came and paid a price for humanity that no one else could pay. It was because of how highly God valued you, His creation.

Acts 15:18 known unto God are all His works from the beginning of the world.

You see, God is not impressed with our abilities, character, obedience, etc. Since He knew us before we were "in our mother's womb", He chose us BEFORE we manifested any of these qualities! He loves us unconditionally. His thoughts toward us are already settled. His only desire is that we fulfill His plan for our lives. The works of God were already completed at the foundation of creation!

Hebrews 4:3-4 *For we which have believed do enter into rest, as he said, As I have sworn in my wrath, if they shall enter into my rest: although the works were finished from the foundation of the world. For he spake in a certain place of the seventh day on this wise, And God did rest the seventh day from all his works.*

Chapter 3

God's Purpose is a Good One

Jeremiah 29:11 For I know the thoughts that I think toward you, saith the LORD, thoughts of peace, and not of evil, to give you an expected end.

<u>Know</u> = this is the same know as "knew" you in the mother's womb. Even His thoughts toward us were already in place before we started in life. We are not changing God's mind by our actions! God does not have any new thoughts about us, but every thought was in place before the world was created. His thoughts about us are only pure, good and righteous. God is not thinking about us as failures. He did not create failures, He created successes!

What kind of thoughts exactly did He have?

<u>Thoughts</u> = device, purposes, plan, calculations, impart

Peace = completeness, soundness, friendship, contentment, finished, in a covenant of peace.

Give = bestow, grant, permit, ascribe, employ, devote, consecrate, dedicate, exchange, lend, commit, entrust, give over, deliver up, yield produce, occasion, produce, requite to, report, mention, utter, stretch out, extend.

Expected = a cord as to bind together. Everything is connected.

End = last or future, an end and expectation

The purposes of God have a future that is bound and woven to the center of our being because of the thoughts He had for us while we were still in the womb and even before our conception. Actually, God created the universe so we could walk out and fulfill His thoughts toward us or what we call our destiny. Imagine the earth was formed just so you could complete God's calculated plan for your life! WOW! Everything I see was created for me to fulfill my destiny. Imagine how much God wants you to succeed. Imagine partnering with Him in life. God, the one who knows the plan, and you, the one who is upon the earth to walk out the plan. You can do nothing but succeed!

Psalm 33:10 The LORD bringeth the counsel of the heathen to nought: he maketh the devices of the people of none effect. The counsel of the LORD standeth for ever, the thought of his heart to all generations.

Counsel = advice and purpose

Standeth = remains, endures.

Thoughts = devices, purposes, plans, calculations.

God's sovereign plan unfolds not only to us but also to all generations! He has a plan for your life and for this generation that is here upon the earth. If enough people fulfill their destiny, the destiny of an entire generation can also come to pass. If for some reason this does not happen, the next generation will fulfill His plan. It is in motion and remains forever, as our destiny is eternal!

19

Isaiah 14:24 The LORD of hosts hath sworn, saying, Surely as I have thought, so shall it come to pass; and as I have purposed, so shall it stand:

Purposed = Counseled, determined

Stand = rise up, come on the scene

Isaiah 55:7-9 Let the wicked forsake his way, and the unrighteous man his thoughts: and let him return unto the LORD, and he will have mercy upon him; and to our God, for he will abundantly pardon. For my thoughts are not your thoughts, neither are your ways my ways, saith the LORD. For as the heavens are higher than the earth, so are my ways higher than your ways, and my thoughts than your thoughts.

Ways = journey, pathway, course of life.

Destiny is seen in God's plan and purposes not ours. Many times our plans and purposes are contrary or lacking in areas because we think in human reasoning and temporal, or in the moment. God thinks concerning the future as well as the present. This is more eternal. This is about going to a higher place to see above our situation. Let's look at some terms we use and may not understand.

Destiny = Destine = What is intended, God's desire toward us, victory, completeness, wholeness, based on our decisions and free will choice.

Destiny is not so much what we do or accomplish, but what we become! What are you becoming with your life?

Foreknowledge = to know before hand. God knows our decisions, responses, and failures.

In *John 18:4*, Jesus knew all things that should come upon Him. This shows that God knows what we should do but does not make the decisions for us. He knows what we have need of and will place things in

21

our path to help us in everyday life. God does not bring hardship or heartache upon us that comes from the devil. He may know something that is evil is about to occur, and if we spend time with Him, we can know these things as well. Recently prophets announced the New Orleans disaster and the Pakistan earthquake days in advance and with great detail. They heard the voice of God. These things are not published in society as a whole but are published in the Christian circles. This proves God would give warning of impending harm. This is foreknowledge. The question is -are we listening?

Another example of this is David and the five stones that he used to kill Goliath. At the time of the earth's creation, these stones were placed in a stream waiting for the day David would make a decision to walk out his destiny. It was part of the thoughts or calculated plan God had for his life. God has set things in place for our destinies as well. Notice it was not merely about David doing something with the stones but more about who he was becoming as he did something with his life. He went from a lowly shepherd boy to the greatest king of Israel. It was about his destiny!

Predestination = to determine before hand, unmovable truths, God's putting in motion of things that are non-negotiable (heaven and hell, salvation by grace through Jesus) A plan for every person on the earth!

Sovereignty = supreme rule, independent from others, not needing help.

Things concerning sovereignty are actually spiritual laws governing the universe and our lives. They are things that our personal decisions have no bearing on. Destiny always has the calling, or God's divine invitation within it!

Romans 8:29-30 *For whom he did foreknow, he also did predestinate to be conformed to the image of his Son, that he might be the firstborn among many brethren. Moreover whom he did predestinate, them he also called: and whom he called, them he also justified: and whom he justified, them he also glorified.*

Formed = fashioned like, to make yourself into another's pattern

Image = a copy or resemblance that is identical to the pattern

Predestinate = to determine before hand

Called = call aloud, utter in a loud voice, to invite, to name

Justified = "be freed", "be righteous" to render righteous, declare, pronounce, one to be just

Glorified = "honor" "have glory" "magnify" "make glorious" to think, suppose, be of opinion, clothe with splendor.

The focus in this section lies upon the action of God — His plan and the accomplishment of His plan. Because God has a plan, or purpose — to sum up all things, to bring all things together in Christ, things in the heaven and things upon earth. He literally is patterning us to resemble Him identically, not only in what we do, but who we will become. By doing this, our destiny is actually connected with a large overall plan God has for the whole earth and not just for us! He desires to take care of us by freeing us from failure, hurts, and disappointments that hinder our destiny. He desires to not only let us experience this plan but to also exalt us in our destiny as it unfolds. This way others can come into destiny because hope has been released. It is one destiny unfolding another person's destiny.

Greg Crawford

Chapter 4

Destiny's Voice

The voice of Destiny is always speaking something either by the drawing of God or the by the one seeking destiny. Paul spoke of how Epaphras prayed fervently for the Church to find the will and purposes of God. Epaphras was a prayer warrior and had God's heart concerning His desire for the Church. *Colossians 4:12 "Epaphras, who is one of you, a servant of Christ, saluteth you, always labouring fervently for you in prayers, that ye may stand perfect and complete in all the will of God"*.

<u>Stand</u> = established, fixed, set, made firm

<u>Perfect</u> = brought to its end, finished, wanting nothing necessary to completeness

<u>Complete</u> = to make full, to fill up, to fill to the full, to cause to abound, to furnish or supply liberally, to

27

render full, to fill to the top: so that nothing shall be wanting, to full measure

God's desire concerning our destiny is that we would find the fullness of it. You will know you have reached this place when you desire nothing else and your life is content. Are you in that place yet? Then keep pursuing God and you will one day find that place. By now, we can begin to see how much God has for us and how much He desires for us to be happy, fulfilled and content with our lives. Even a young adult can have this experience as well.

The will of God for your life works out three distinct things:

Stand: Spiritual Foundation, Spiritual
                Understanding

Perfect: Spiritual Satisfaction

Complete: Spiritual Abundance, Spiritual Flow

The will of God being fulfilled also hinges on our heart attitude and openness. God's will and our destiny and purpose will never be found in programs or books but actually flows out of our heart or spirit, and is focused on service to God and not to man. Even the great King David, said he was first a king to God and then to the people. Apostle Paul, who wrote much of the New Testament, discovered this also.

Ephesians 6:6-7 Not with eye service, as men pleasers; but as the servants of Christ, doing the will of God from the heart; 7 With good will doing service, as to the Lord, and not to men:

Doing = to make, with the names of things made, to produce, construct, form, fashion, etc., to be the authors of, the cause to make ready, to prepare, to produce, bear, shoot forth

From = preposition denoting origin (the point whence action or motion proceeds)

Heart = breath, the breath of life, the vital force which animates the body and shows itself in breathing, that

29

in which there is life

The will of God always flows from the heart of God and connects with our heart.

> **2 Corinthians 1:1, Colossians 1:1, 1 Corinthians 1:1, John 4:34, Romans 1:10, Romans 8:27**

As our heart is engaged with the Lord, we can easily begin to see God's intentions and plan for us. God says it is not based on our natural talents or the ability of our mind to comprehend, but the will of God is spiritual and we as spiritual beings can know and understand it!

Ephesians 5:16-20 Redeeming the time, because the days are evil. 17 Wherefore be ye not unwise, but understanding what the will of the Lord is. 18 And be not drunk with wine, wherein is excess; but be filled with the Spirit; 19 Speaking to yourselves in psalms and hymns and spiritual songs, singing and making melody in your heart to the Lord; 20 Giving thanks always for all things unto God and the Father in the name of our Lord Jesus Christ;

<u>**Understanding**</u> = to set or bring together, to put (as it were) the perception with the thing perceived

__Will__ = Pleasure, desire, have in mind, intend

The will of God is not your position, but it is your function! God's will actually brings Him pleasure when it comes into focus. You can actually move His heart as you fulfill the will of God. God is concerned how you act, not what role you play. We see this in Jesus. While He was on the earth, He made three distinct confessions:

1.   Who He was

2.   What He was sent to do

3.   What the overall mission was

These confessions kept the will of God in the forefront and made people aware that God has a plan for humanity. He completed the will of God for His life and we can complete the will of God for our lives.

John 17:4 I have glorified thee on the earth: I have finished the work which thou gavest me to do.

Jesus' destiny of dying on the cross and completing

the will of God concerning His life now enables us to fulfill the destiny God has for our lives! Sometimes we are trying to figure things out with our minds instead of being led by the Spirit. We have to reach a point of ceasing from our struggles so we can enter into the rest of God concerning our lives.

***Hebrews 4:3** For we which have believed do enter in rest, as he said, As I have sworn in my wrath, if they shall enter into my rest: although the works were finished from the foundation of the world.*

<u>Work</u>s = an act, deed, thing done: undertaking

<u>Finished</u> = come to pass, to come into existence, begin to be, to arise, appear in history, of miracles, to be performed.

As far as God is concerned, the works were finished at the very time they started. This is true faith.

We should expect that we will finish everything we start. God expects us to finish or accomplish His will in our lives and we should be filled with the same expectation.

Destiny is really only an extension of Jesus' destiny!

2 Timothy 1:9-10 *Who hath saved us, and called us with an holy calling, not according to our works, but according to his own purpose and grace, which was given us in Christ Jesus before the world began, But is now made manifest by the appearing of our Saviour Jesus Christ, who hath abolished death, and hath brought life and immortality to light through the gospel:*

Called = call aloud or command

Calling = invitation, vocation

Purpose = setting forth, placing into view, place before

The call of God is a divine invitation to a specific destiny. This invitation has within it the ability to perform the tasks required within the destiny. The calling, grace and purpose were all in place in Jesus Christ before the world began. Already, we have seen how our lives and God's plan have existed together. The world was created just for you to fulfill the plan of God. He also has given us His favor and even sets into view His desires for us! WOW! Imagine

33

everything has already been done for us. No wonder Jesus said it is finished at the cross. Not only was salvation complete, but also destiny was loosed into our lives at that very moment.

Romans 12:2 *And be not conformed to this world: but be ye transformed by the renewing of your mind, that ye may prove what is that good, and acceptable, and perfect, will of God.*

Prove = to test, examine, prove, to recognize as genuine (what we do concerning God's will)

Good = good constitution or nature, upright, honorable (What the will of God's nature is)

Acceptable = well pleasing, to prosper, agreeable (What it does for us)

Perfect = brought to its end, finished, wanting nothing necessary to completeness

Root = termination, the limit at which a thing ceases to be, always of the end of some act or state, but not of the end of a period of time (<u>The finished result</u>)

There are not degrees of the will of God but only one

level of the will of God. The other sections in this verse tell us our role, what the will accomplishes and the finished result. Many of us never start the journey to know our destiny unless we see it completely. But the truth of the matter is that we will not know the will of God until we have completed the task or assignment God has placed before us. We do this by first taking a step of faith. It is only afterward that we can truly look back and see that the steps we have taken in our lives were the will of God all along. We need to keep walking by faith, moving forward and doing the will of God from our heart and thus we release our destiny by faith.

The will of God is not about us but about Jesus Christ and His plan and Kingdom. It is not about our individual ministry but the corporate Body of Christ. There are not varying degrees of the will of God. Either something is the will of God or it is not the will of God. We are saved or not saved, healed or not healed. There is no half way. There is no in-between. There is no gray area with God.

Greg Crawford

Chapter 5

Closure of the Past to
Release Destiny in the Present

We will never find our destiny by looking at our past failures. We constantly look backward and see how we should have changed things or we say, "If I had just…" The thing to realize is **God never took someone backward to go forward**. Our destiny is not behind us but is in our future before us. However, closure of the past is important. Most people never move to a new season because they refuse to close the past or even their current season of life. Closing one age always opens the next.

Acts 3:21 *Whom the heaven must receive until the times of restitution of all things, which God hath spoken by the mouth of all his holy prophets since the world began.*

The time of restitution or restoration of all things is now. If you feel your destiny has been taken from you, God desires to restore your hope and see your destiny fulfilled. Your destiny is still intact, hidden in the heart of God. He is protecting it for you until you can fully possess it.

Ecclesiastes 3:1 *To every thing there is a season, and a time to every purpose under the heaven:*

The word **season** means a fixed time. It also states it is towards every purpose under heaven. The word **purpose** means an experience, event, and comes from a root word meaning 'to advance'. God has a plan to take you to the next season so that you can actually see the purpose of God in your life. That means even the current season, no matter how good it is, will be replaced with a greater season that is coming your way. Remember if purpose and grace existed before the world began, that same grace is there to enable you to leave the past and stretch towards the future.

John 19:30 *When Jesus therefore had received the vinegar, he said, It is finished: and he bowed his head, and gave up the ghost.*

Jesus closed the season of law so that the season of grace would begin. We celebrate an end, the cross, to exist into the future of grace. We need to celebrate the end of what is behind us and be excited about what is before us.

Several people had to make the same decisions before they entered into destiny and did great things for God. In *1 King 19:16* Elijah called out Elisha and he left everything to follow him, closing one season and opening another. Job was a man who had to close a season to open another. *Luke 18:22* Jesus told the rich young man to sell all and follow Him, starting a new season in life. *John 1:43* Jesus told Phillip to come follow Him. *Mark 2:14* Jesus told Matthew to leave all and come follow Him. Jesus told John and Peter to follow Him. They left a season of their lives to go with Him, yet returned to their previous season after Jesus died. They realized they had to leave it again in order to move forward into the next season of Church history.

Leaving your past may mean to break off friendships that are unproductive. It may mean leaving old concepts of Christian life, or even attractive distractions. It also means to leave false dreams and visions that we know God has never intended for our lives. <u>It will mean to make faith decisions and not emotional decisions.</u> It means we put our lives under Jesus' Lordship and trust Him with our lives and future. After all, every destiny was released after a decision to follow God and His ways was made. We step by faith into the future knowing it holds our destiny.

This process is sometimes painful. Even Jesus had to come to grips with His death for the next season to come to humanity. We also need to deal with the past season that is closing to allow the next season to come to us in our Christian life.

So what really stops us from closing seasons in our lives? The main thing is becoming too comfortable with where we are and holding it at a greater value than our future.

Hebrews 4:1-3 Let us therefore fear, lest, a promise being left us of entering into his rest, any of you should seem to come short of it. 2 For unto us was the gospel preached, as well as unto them: but the word preached did not profit them, not being mixed with faith in them that heard it. 3 For we which have believed do enter into rest, as he said, As I have sworn in my wrath, if they shall enter into my rest: although the works were finished from the foundation of the world.

Things that can hinder us:

1. Fear of the future

    a. False illusions of what is coming

    b. False hope and false faith being exercised

2. Attachments from the past that we have not released. We cannot bring what could have been, into the present.

3. Rest will not come unless we have closed the past.

4. An unfinished past always brings frustration to the present.

Hebrews 4:9-11 *There remaineth therefore a rest to the people of God. 10 For he that is entered into his rest, he also hath ceased from his own works, as God did from his. 11 Let us labour therefore to enter into that rest, lest any man fall after the same example of unbelief.*

5. Ceasing from your own works to do God's work.

6. Unbelief that a new season is coming, bringing new ways.

When do we have closure?

- When we have rest
- When we are settled on the Word of the Lord for us
- When we are more in faith than feelings
- When we have a great sense of purpose in God

Chapter 6

Pursuit to Bring an Encounter

We can't just sit and wait thinking our destiny will suddenly appear. It takes putting our faith into action. We need to be focused more on the overall picture, than the day- to-day specifics. Sometimes the specifics can sidetrack us, even weigh us down, and we lose track of where we are going. Even our prayer lives may change as we start our pursuit. We need life-changing encounters rather than just praying for our needs. After all, He already promised to supply them. It is seeing things with a larger mindset and starting to dream about the unlimited possibilities that rest in God. Paul gives the best example of what he did to reach his destiny.

Philippians 3:10-15 That I may know him, and the power of his resurrection, and the fellowship of his sufferings, being made conformable unto his death; 11 If by any means I might attain unto the resurrection of the dead. 12 Not as though I had already attained, neither were already perfect: but I follow after, if that I may apprehend that for which also I am apprehended of Christ Jesus. 13 Brethren, I count not myself to have apprehended: but this one thing I do, forgetting those things which are behind, and reaching forth unto those things which are before, 14 I press toward the mark for the prize of the high calling of God in Christ Jesus.15 Let us therefore, as many as be perfect, be thus minded: and if in any thing ye be otherwise minded, God shall reveal even this unto you.

Look at the tremendous meaning of the word 'apprehend'!

Apprehend = to lay hold of so as to make one's own, to obtain, attain to, to make one's own, to take into one's self, appropriate, to lay hold of with the mind Root word = to take with the hand, lay hold of, any person or thing in order to use it.

What or how was Paul apprehended? It was in *Acts 9* when the Lord appeared to him. It was an attitude of his heart that decided, no matter what, he had to attain the provision of the Lord's intimacy. You see God always puts a desire in us to seek Him even before we desire to seek after Him! All we have to do is pursue, and when we reach Him, yield. Paul said God apprehended him and this encounter made Paul wanting to be apprehended by God.

There are six <u>prerequisites</u> to any encounter:

Hebrews 11:6 But without faith it is impossible to please him: for he that cometh to God must believe that he is, and that he is a rewarder of them that diligently seek him.

1. Faith

2. Come to God, not men

3. Must believe

4. Must believe He will reward your efforts

5. Must be diligent

6. Must seek HIM!

Paul did all of these prior to his encounter on the Damascus road. Even though Paul did some things wrong that were detrimental to the Christian faith, he was still pursuing, as misguided as it was. You see,

God honors the actions of attempting and trying over the inactivity of sitting and doing nothing.

Deuteronomy 4:29 *But if from thence thou shalt seek the LORD thy God, thou shalt find him, if thou seek him with all thy heart and with all thy soul.*

This is a Promise!

Seek = desire, request, make demand

Find = attain, secure, find out

Chapter 7

Three "One Things"

Once we decide to pursue, we have to stay focused on three "One Things".

1. Seeking Him

Psalm 27:4 *One thing have I desired of the LORD, that will I seek after; that I may dwell in the house of the LORD all the days of my life, to behold the beauty of the LORD, and to enquire in his temple.*

<u>Desired</u> = crave, demand

David spoke this just after he finished talking about the enemies in his life. He was not focused on circumstance but on his relationship with God. David actually went seven times a day to the tabernacle to inquire of the Lord. He was drawn by the grace of God and the need to find out more about who God was and what David's destiny was within His plan for humanity. This grace enabled him not only to see

47

into the beauty realm of God, but also to prioritize his life. David's abiding and dwelling in the tabernacle was more than just casual inquiry. It was diligent seeking and this act encompasses all six prerequisites for encounter with God. David learned that unbroken communion with God will keep you from falling into sin! He realized that every holy urge requires cooperation.

2. Sitting at Jesus' Feet

Luke 10:38-42 *Now it came to pass, as they went, that he entered into a certain village: and a certain woman named Martha received him into her house. 39 And she had a sister called Mary, which also sat at Jesus' feet, and heard his word. 40 But Martha was cumbered about much serving, and came to him, and said, Lord, dost thou not care that my sister hath left me to serve alone? bid her therefore that she help me. 41 And Jesus answered and said unto her, Martha, Martha, thou art careful and troubled about many things: 42 But one thing is needful: and Mary hath chosen that good part, which shall not be taken away from her.*

We must take time out of our busy schedules and sit at the feet of Jesus. Every time someone has gone to this place of humility, something happened that affected his or her life. People were healed (*Matt 15:30, Luke 17:16*), delivered (*Mark 7:25*), or even rose from the dead (*Luke 8:42*). Jesus himself said it was the one thing that was needful!

Psalm 37:4 Delight thyself also in the LORD; and he shall give thee the desires of thine heart.

Delight = to make merry and be happy over

Give = to deliver, set or grant

Desires = requests and petitions

Our sin and actions do not surprise God. After all, He made a provision for it. What surprises Him is our lack of desire to be with Him. His presence is the only solution to lack. When we take time out to be with Him, it changes the things around us. The times of coming short fade away and are replaced with the glory of God being revealed in our lives. The question that so many have had to answer in the examples above is: Can you still take time and come sit at His feet even though you know you have failed, even though you have been in sin or are feeling unworthy? The truth is, in spite of your mistakes, this is the most crucial time to come and be with Him. These are the times He will draw close to you and remind you of the real destiny you have and not the false one trying to crowd into your life.

3. Forgetting the Past

Paul, of all people, realized how an unholy past could grip a person's destiny. He had to make a determination, being the worst of sinners, that it would not dictate his future. Yesterday is already gone, good or bad, and nothing can change it. But the future is before us. How are we spending our thoughts towards what is ahead?

Philippians 3:7-15 *But what things were gain to me, those I counted loss for Christ. 8 Yea doubtless, and I count all things but loss for the excellency of the knowledge of Christ Jesus my Lord: for whom I have suffered the loss of all things, and do count them but dung, that I may win Christ, 9 And be found in him, not having mine own righteousness, which is of the law, but that which is through the faith of Christ, the righteousness which is of God by faith: 10 That I may know him, and the power of his resurrection, and the fellowship of his sufferings, being made conformable unto his death; 11 If by any means I might attain unto the resurrection of the dead. 12 Not as though I had already attained, either were already perfect: but I follow after, if that I may apprehend that for which also I am apprehended of Christ Jesus. 13 Brethren, I count not myself to have apprehended: but this one thing I do, forgetting those things which are behind, and reaching forth unto those things which are before, 14 I press toward the mark for the prize of the high calling of God in Christ Jesus. 15 Let us therefore, as many as be perfect, be thus minded: and if in any thing ye be otherwise minded, God shall reveal even this unto you.*

Paul says everything was loss except one thing, "knowing Christ". This is not a casual 'knowing', but intimate knowledge of being with Him. Paul said he wanted to be found in Him. Paul saw his past as something HE had to let go of. God was not holding it against him now or in the future. Paul could not hold himself back, either. He saw that the only thing he needed to do was stretch forth towards the destiny God had for him. When Paul experienced the forgiveness, grace and purpose of God, he had no choice but to be apprehended. The prize that he saw far outweighed the cost of getting there and he valued it more than his current condition.

Chapter 8

Steps to Fulfilling the Purposes of God

1. Get a revelation and conviction concerning whether or not you are truly connected to the present truth and if you and that truth are meant for each other.

- Do your desires, vision and theology connect with God's present move?

- Are you willing to seek God for new vision and leave the old?

- Make sure the revelation of your ministry is clear to the Body of Christ in order to be able to fulfill it.

2. Make a covenant with God that you will stay within His purpose and destiny for your life regardless of how it affects your life.

- Become a prisoner to the purpose of God

53

- Full revelation will not come unless you are fully committed to see that revelation manifest

- You must begin working out your destiny without seeing the full picture.

3. Maintain close relationship with Jesus Christ until the truth and purpose within you fills you and you are 'pregnant' with destiny

- Revelation is birthed in intimacy

- Destiny is the revealing of God's heart and you aligning with His purpose in His heart

4. Keep your faith active and keep confidence in God that He will perform the destiny and plan in your life.

- Do not abandon what has been started even if it gets hard or you do not understand

- God is the only one who truly understands and sees what is going on inside of you.

- God knows when it is time to give birth to

destiny

- *Isaiah 66:1-10*

- Make sure you are fully restored and healthy

5. Allow God to bring you to the point of delivering your destiny for others to see.

- Realize the chronos (chronological) time will change to the kairos (God's appointed) time in God

- Do not force premature birth

- Let the Holy Spirit lead the birthing time and process

- Trust God, He will get you through

- Realize it will be a painful process

6. Nurture your destiny until mature

- Adjust your priorities and schedule to nurture

your destiny.

- Become equipped properly with what skills you will need.

Chapter 9

Examples of Those Who Fulfilled Destiny

Isaiah 55:11 So shall my word be that goeth forth out of my mouth: it shall not return unto me void, but it shall accomplish that which I please, and it shall prosper in the thing whereto I sent it.

When the Word goes forth, it calls forth destiny out of the individual believer's life and into fulfillment! It is God's thoughts in action towards us. Thoughts that only He has, but we then openly see! Of the 400 men and women who started in the Bible, only 80 finished strong. We need to be those who will finish our purpose and destiny. Here are a few for study. Let us see what they faced and who they became (destiny).

Abraham

Gave up: His family, land, etc., his past for a future (*Genesis 12*)

Promise: Father of many nations (*Gen. 15:5*)

Problem: For a time was not fully persuaded (*Rom. 4:21*)

Destiny: Righteousness

Joseph

Gave up: Family and heritage

Promise: That he would be exalted to a position of authority (*Genesis 37*)

Problem: Imprisoned, forsaken, etc.

Destiny: Saved Israel

Moses

Gave up: Egypt, then lived a life of solitude (*Ex. 4*)

Promise: To be a deliverer (*Ex. 4*)

Problem: His own self and shortcomings (*Ex. 4*)

Destiny: Israel delivered and positioned to enter their promise

Gideon

Gave up: Fear and frustration for promise, "Mighty man of valor" (*Judges 6*)

Promise: To free Israel from the attacks of the enemy

Problem: All odds against him - - 300 mighty men

Destiny: To prove the depth of faith in God

Nehemiah

Gave up: Position of cupbearer

Promise: Only a burden in his heart (Nehemiah)

Problem: No way possible to fulfill his burden unless God intervened

Destiny: Rebuilding the walls; because of this, Ezra could build upon his destiny. He rebuilt the people of God! Purpose always focuses on people!

David

Gave up: Fear of not being chosen (*1 Chron. 14:2* – perceived to be a king)

Promise: To be King and establish the dwelling of God

Problem: Waiting for office to come

Destiny: To build a dwelling place for God (*Amos 9; Acts 15:16* – not outward pattern, but inward relationship

Jonah

Gave up: Self-righteous attitude

<u>Promise</u>:   Voice of deliverance (Jonah)

Problem: His attitude

<u>Destiny</u>:   To bring Nineveh to repentance

Peter

Gave up: Everything

<u>Promise</u>:   "Upon this rock I will build my church" (*Matthew 16:18*)

Problem: Ongoing failures

<u>Destiny</u>:   Father of the Church

Jesus

Gave up: Heaven

<u>Promise</u>:   The Kingdom of God established on earth

Problem: Rejected by the people He was to save

Destiny: To be our deliverer and make us victorious

You

Give up: Self by laying your life down

Promise: To be more than a conqueror

Problem: Your own self-will

Destiny: To establish the Kingdom, fulfill God's will, and walk in victory!

I trust this short study has helped you to realize purposes are what we do, and destiny is truly what we become. If you are a young adult, you have your entire life before you. I cannot stress enough the urgency that you find your destiny as soon as possible. You need to understand how God has made you and what gifting He has placed inside of you. They are unique to you and they all show forth your destiny. I also hope you now see the thoughts God has towards you and how you were in the very heart of God before the world was created. May you take time out to sit at Jesus' feet, forget your past, and realize as you peer into the heart of God, you are peering into your future and destiny as well!

Chapter 10

Finding Your Identity

One of the primary things needed above all other things is for us to know our identity. I am not talking about who others tell us we are but who God says we are. One of the main things young people face today is their identity. They are told by others who they are. They are forced and pressured into being someone they know deep down inside they really are not. But to "fit in" they have to take on this new identity and out of that, behave or function a certain way to be part of the crowd.

Once a young person leaves high school and goes to college, the standard line is "they really don't know what they are going to do with their life". This is not because of not making choices but because their identity has left them. They graduated and all their classmates went different directions after high school. Their identity left as well. The quarterback, cheerleader, or most popular person is no longer. That identity has left and so until they get a new identity, vacillation occurs. It is not about

63

sorting out what to do because you only function out of your identity. In high school, you functioned to get an identity that is why it left at graduation. There was no place to function anymore.

So the need arises for a person to find their true identity. This is only going to be realized if they hear what their Creator says about them. The world's way is to function to get your identity. God's way is for you to get identity so you can function. The best way to get God's identity for you is to hear what He says about you. There are conversations going on right now in heaven about you!

Philippians 3:17-21

17 Brethren, be followers together of me, and mark them which walk so as ye have us for an ensample. 18 (For many walk, of whom I have told you often, and now tell you even weeping, that they are the enemies of the cross of Christ: 19 Whose end is destruction, whose God is their belly, and whose glory is in their shame, who mind earthly things.) 20 For our conversation is in heaven; from whence also we look for the Saviour, the Lord Jesus Christ: 21 Who shall change our vile body, that it may be fashioned like unto his glorious body, according to the working whereby he is able even to subdue all things unto himself.

The word 'conversation' means the administration of civil affairs or of a commonwealth and the commonwealth of citizens. God has conversations about these areas for humanity with those that are listening upon earth today. Also, these conversations are about us as individuals and what we will accomplish in our lives. It's about tuning in to heaven and listening to what He is saying about us. The first step is reading the Word of God to gain perspective of what God is saying, or already has said about us in His Word. Let's look at a real example that shows God is talking about us in heaven.

Luke 1:26-30

26 And in the sixth month the angel Gabriel was sent from God unto a city of Galilee, named Nazareth , 27 To a virgin espoused to a man whose name was Joseph, of the house of David; and the virgin's name was Mary . 28 And the angel came in unto her, and said, Hail, thou that art highly favoured, the Lord is with thee: blessed art thou among women . 29 And when she saw him , she was troubled at his saying, and cast in her mind what manner of salutation this should be . 30 And the angel said unto her, Fear not, Mary: for thou hast found favour with God .

The angel in verse 28 told Mary she is highly favored. This is not the angel's opinion, it is God's opinion. The angel is simply a messenger repeating what he has already been told. He literally is repeating a conversation that occurred in heaven as God was talking about the favor that would rest upon Mary. It is more than just a declaration of this favor, I believe there was a lengthy conversation in heaven concerning just how far this favor would reach.

Mary responded like so many of us when we are confronted with our identity. She responded in fear unsure of what this favor could actually mean. She was trying to figure it out in her mind, but God speaks to our hearts. The angel confronts her fear in verse 30 and tells her that she has found favor. He is speaking that it is in the past tense and has already occurred. In other words, God has already decided and she is now being notified.

The angel described the favor that rested upon her life. Mary actually started getting her new identity. She is highly favored and blessed among women. He described that she will be known as the one who birthed the Son of God into the earth.

God desires that we would hear what He is saying about us in heaven. It's obvious the angel heard a conversation in heaven and was sent to the earth to tell Mary. Right now there are conversations going on in heaven about you. God is speaking to angels and the heavenly host and declaring all the great exploits you will do with your life. He is declaring how your life will count and matter upon the earth. He is telling what will come forth from your life and how it will affect others.

You see, until we settle our identity, we will not be able to conceive what God has for us. How do we hear what God is saying about us in heaven? It is through intimacy. Intimacy is what releases our identity. Intimacy allows us to truly hear what God is saying about us. When we accept our identity from God is the point of conception of our destiny. Just like Mary had to make a decision that she would receive the identity God was presenting. When she did, she conceived by the Holy Spirit. When Mary visited Elizabeth, the fruit of her identity, Jesus, her unborn son, impacted Elizabeth's spirit and a babe leaped in the womb. God desires that the identity we have in Him be so sure, so settled, that it would conceive inside of us something so precious when others are around it, they will be impacted as well.

Chapter 11

Identity Formed in the Glory

Every time we enter into God's Glory we should expect something to be encountered. When we are in God's glory, we release our faith more easily. It is the place we can hear what God says about us and also the place our identity is realized. Once we settle our identity, it will only remain if captured in God's glory!

As wonderful as our experiences in God are, they do not define our identity. They are only expressions of it. Otherwise we let anointing identify us or we let experiences or physical manifestations identify us. God wants His glory to identify us!!

Isaiah 62:1-3

¹ For Zion's sake will I not hold my peace, and for Jerusalem's sake I will not rest, until the righteousness thereof go forth as brightness, and the salvation thereof as a lamp that burneth . ² And the Gentiles shall see thy righteousness, and all kings thy glory: and thou shalt be called by a new name, which the mouth of the LORD shall name . ³ Thou shalt also be a crown of glory in the hand of the LORD, and a royal diadem in the hand of thy God.

The word 'new' means a freshness. It is also used for non-material things as name (*Is. 62:2*), song (*Ps. 149:1*), covenant (*Jer 31:31*), God's mercies (*Lam 3:23*), heart, and spirit (*Ezek. 36:26*). While suffering, Job longed for the time when His glory was "fresh" in him (*Job 29:20*).   You see God desires to give you a new name or a fresh name. It is as if He wants you to have a new beginning that He has decided and declared over you.

Moses asked the question in *Ex. 3:11*. He said, "Who am I." He did not know and was unsure that God would allow him this honor of encounter. The first thing in the encounter dealt deep inside to exactly who he was before God, not before men. Before men, he knew who he was, but now God Himself challenged him.

Your first encounter with your identity is in the encounter with the God of identity. You have to first settle the issue of who God is in your life to settle the issue of who God says you are in His life! This type of encounter is in God's realm not ours. What God reveals about your assignments is also a revealing of the identity needed to fulfill them. What God promises you exposes you to what your identity will open in the spirit realm. Moses was told he would be a deliverer (identity) called to deliver (function) an entire nation. He functioned out of his identity and only after he had an encounter with God to receive his true identity. It was like he was hiding from God's identity for his life for 40 years. No matter how hard we try to remain hidden from it, God will bring the reality of what He is saying before our ears to hear!

God has a way of speaking to us that leads us to our identity. We all know that Abraham had his name changed at one point in his life. In *Genesis 15:1*, Abraham had an encounter with God. Within five verses, he received a promise from God. Within 18 verses, he had a covenant with God. But in *Genesis 17: 1*, he received a new name and a new identity. This name is a reflection of what he will accomplish of being the father of many nations. He is changed

71

from Abram to Abraham. Abram means exalted father, while Abraham means Father of a multitude. At 99 years old, he received a new identity. It is never too late for you to pursue your identity.

What stops identity from coming in?

Some of the things that stop our identity from coming to us are that we don't fully believe in God's promises. We see ourselves as inadequate or not worthy to enter into what God has spoken over our lives. Just like Abraham, if we do not accept God's promises for us, we will never fulfill our destiny and come into our identity.

Like others in the Bible, perhaps we do not want to accept or complete the assignments that God has given to us. But the thing is every assignment that God gives us is leading us to our identity. Assignments form and reveal who we really are. Assignments that we have not fulfilled or completed are actually parts of our lives where we don't understand who we really are. This may keep us from accepting God's identity for our life because we have not chosen to fulfill the assignments He has given us.

Sometimes our identity seems far away and distant because we have distanced ourselves and not positioned ourselves in God's covenant. This covenant enables us to stay within boundaries to see God's promise, assignments, and His identity for us fulfilled. When we step outside of covenant, we have stepped outside of boundaries that God has placed in our life. At that place, we are outside of the true identity of what He has called us to be.

Probably one of the hardest things for us to accept is that God always gives us an identity that is greater than we see ourselves. It is not thinking more highly of ourselves than we should, but it is accepting how God thinks about us and understanding the potential that He sees lying within each of us. In all honesty, we actually do not have a right to look upon ourselves as less than what He has declared over us. Just like Abraham had to come to the conclusion that God could see the beginning to the end. What was ahead in his future was only known by the God that

73

he followed. We also are like this and wrestle with this just as much as Abraham did. We try to sort out and figure out our identity and how we will fulfill covenant and promises that God has given us. The only way to truly find identity is to rest in God's covenant, fulfill His promises, and accept what He truly says about us.

Mount of Transfiguration   *Luke 9*

On the Mount of Transfiguration, Jesus wants to show Peter, James and John how the glory will change their identity. In verse *28*, they are given an assignment to pray. Jesus knew this assignment would keep them focused and fine-tune their spirits to hear what the Father was saying in that moment. But like so many, they abandoned the assignment and fell asleep. It almost seems like a parallel of the Church today. But we see something interesting that happens to Jesus.

In verse *29*, as Jesus prayed He was changed from the inside and out. He had entered into the glory realm of God. This realm so affected His identity that His appearance was changed. This is one of the things that happen when we know our identity; our outward appearance is changed.

In the midst of the story, Jesus' identity is once again released in the midst of the glory of God. Others heard His voice as the Father spoke. In verse 35, Jesus' identity is once again reinforced. The Father speaks and says "this is my beloved Son, hear him". The Glory of God always has the sound of His voice within it and His voice is always speaking our identity.

Jesus had taken the three men up the Mount on an assignment of prayer. The assignment was for them to also see His identity, and to realize the importance of them finding their identity. These three men's lives were impacted in Scripture after they truly understood their identity.

Peter saw an identity of a carrier of the Glory that later would release healing from his shadow. James saw an identity of God's foundation of His Word being established and he became the first father of the

Church. John saw the identity of Christ and God that transcends earthly limitations and this enabled him to see into the revelatory realm.

All three men saw the same thing but all three received parts of their identity differently. Our identity is only an extension of Jesus' identity. In other words, our identity is only a small part or carries a small degree of the glory of His identity. When man was made in the image of God, he was not made just having some attributes, but was made carrying an identity to reflect the glory of the Lord. Once we see our identity, then we begin to function out of that identity and we become the reflection that God had intended our lives to be.

Peter's identity is a transitional identity or having a transitional function. He preached the first message at Pentecost and transitioned out of the time of Christ upon the earth to the Spirit upon the earth. Peter was the one who was chosen to transition the Church to the Gentiles. He was also the one who was released from prison and transitioned the Church again to reach out into the uttermost parts of the world. All these actions coming into his life are only extensions of his identity.

James' identity is more foundational in function and expression. He became the father of the Church in Jerusalem and led the Church after it transitioned with Peter. He led the first apostolic council in *Acts 15*. He was also the one who wrote the letters to the churches so the entire body of Christ at that time had complete understanding of new doctrines. Once again, his function is coming out of his identity.

John's identity is more revelatory. John saw the end of Jerusalem in the coming of Christ at 70 AD. When John's life appeared to be ended and of no more value, he then began to see the same revelation that Jesus Christ did. You see even when it appears that we have run the race and completed all things, our identity continues to speak and bring forth expressions of function out of our lives.

All three of these identities also worked together as a team because they were working as an extension of the glory of God. All three knew when the other identity was to lead. It was not about personalities but the personality of Christ being expressed through their identities. All jealousy was gone and the ability to step aside for the sake of the Body came solely out

77

of the comprehension and settledness of the identity each one held.

One of the greatest examples of someone who has been changed and given a new identity is the apostle Paul. While on the road to Damascus, he had his encounter in the glory of God. His identity was released to him that he had been searching for his entire life. Paul had been functioning out of what everyone else had told him he really was. He had not settled the issues of his own heart but allowed others to dictate them to him. But on that Damascus Road when the glory of God engulfed him, God began to speak to Saul releasing his identity to him.

Saul's name was changed from 'one desired' to Paul meaning 'small or little'. At the point of Paul's encounter, God had already determined a new identity for him. He would send portions of it into Paul's life when he transitioned into the Christian walk.

In this instance, we see that God called upon a man by the name of Ananias who He would use as a spokesman to further reveal Paul's identity.

Acts 9:11-12 And the Lord said unto him, Arise, and go into the street which is called Straight, and enquire in the house of Judas for one called Saul, of Tarsus: for, behold, he prayeth , 12 And hath seen in a vision a man named Ananias coming in, and putting his hand on him, that he might receive his sight .

God was not looking at Saul and his identity or what others have said he was to be. God has settled the identity of each of us like he settled the identity he had for Paul. Paul's sight was held back from him because this too, would be part of his identity. He would need to look to the eyes of God and know that God was a miracle working God as he walked through life and was put into extreme situations. This conversion was also a conversion of his identity and his function at the same time. Like so many in the Bible, the way of conversion so many times reflects what is required of the person through their life.

Acts 9:15-16 But the Lord said unto him, Go thy way: <u>for he is a chosen vessel unto me, to bear my name</u> before the Gentiles, and kings, and the children of Israel : 16 For I will shew him how great things he must suffer for my name's sake .

God told Ananias that part of Paul's identity was to also bear His name. All would have to come to grips that he was to be a total reflection of who God was in his life. Yet at this point, God does not give Saul a new name. He would have to walk out his salvation with fear and trembling, improve himself, and then he would be able to bear the name of the Lord. Like Abraham, he would have to learn the promises of God and walk in the covenant of God before his name would be changed.

Acts 11:26 ⁶ And when he had found him, he brought him unto Antioch. And it came to pass, that a whole year they assembled themselves with the church, and taught much people. And the disciples were called Christians first in Antioch.

One of the privileges that Saul had is that he was present when the Church was given its first identity. Not only were they called disciples, they were also called Christians at Antioch. This identity still holds true with the Church today, except it is used very loosely. Most believe that by having the name 'Christian', it implies spiritual status. That may not be true. This is why so many are upset with the hypocrisy of the Church and its members. They are called one thing, or have an identity, but the identity does not reflect the functions and actions of one who is called a Christian. It's amazing to me that the world can so easily see it and yet we cannot police ourselves. We allow false identities to be easily spoken thus causing much confusion in the minds of unbelievers.

The Church is to be moving from glory to glory not anointing to anointing. Anointing is the divine enablement of God. The glory of God is where identity is truly found. God moves us from one understanding of our identity to a deeper understanding of our identity. We are actually moving from past identities to future identities. Once we get into heaven, we'll even receive another new identity, a new name will be given unto us.

Revelation 2:17[7] He that hath an ear, let him hear what the Spirit saith unto the churches; To him that overcometh will I give to eat of the hidden manna, and will give him a white stone, and in the stone a new name written, which no man knoweth saving he that receiveth it .

The word "new" means something fresh, recently

made, one-of-a-kind, uncommon, unheard of, and unprecedented. In other words we will get a name or an identity that has never been seen or used at any time!

Chapter 12

Removing the Cloudiness of Your Future

Many of us today realize that we have a future in God. However, when we see our future and we see our reality, the two do not seem to be the same.

What exactly is the future? The future is actually the revelation of God specifically to our life. When revelation comes, prophecy comes, or we have dreams and visions. We are actually experiencing types of revelation concerning our future. Revelation received is the future revealed. The early Church moved based on revelation and not circumstance. As we look to those in the Book of Acts, we see that they first got a revelation and then acted upon that revelation, bringing God's intentions or future into the present. This created a dynamic life in the Spirit with tremendous results capturing the hearts of men. Revelation always releases our future and produces a testimony in our lives.

83

Revelation for your life is revealed in three areas: your personal life and walk, your corporate life in the Body, and God's plan for the earth and how you fit into that plan. The first thing we need to do is look at the revelation that we have been given for our future and see which of these three areas does that revelation actually fit. To gain more revelation, or the revealing of our future, it goes like this:

TIME   with Jesus   Personal revelation

TIME   with Holy Spirit   Corporate revelation
        TIME   with the Father   Plan for the earth

Every leader in the Bible had a revelation of his life first, how it fit in the corporate body second, and God's plan on the earth. Revelation is usually not about you but what you do partnering with God. It is about being a steward of your future until you own your destiny. God is looking for those who can embrace their future to release the future of others.

We are living in the season of the Lord's advancement and release of the future. Prophetic words are held in the balance and some are waiting for the manifestations of the sons of God. Some revelations cannot come because people are not yet in a place to receive them. Others are unfolding quickly. Those who have embraced revelation and are coming into their future will be those God uses as His instruments to bring revelation and reformation.

You see revelation impregnates us with what God desires to conceive on the earth. Revelation always produces Glory. When we look at Acts, we see a pattern of revelation that came to Moses' life.

Revelation of the future always produces increase and multiplication

Acts 7:17-18

¹⁷ But when the time of the promise drew nigh, which God had sworn to Abraham, the people grew and multiplied in Egypt , ¹⁸ Till another king arose, which knew not Joseph .

What was happening was a promise given to Abraham had not yet been fulfilled. But the promise was drawing near. In other words, part of Abraham's future was about to manifest on the earth. This promise, yet 400 years old, was going to affect an entire nation! So God, in His wisdom, brought increase and multiplication of the number of those who would be affected by the promise. What is coming will affect every person, backslidden, prodigal, unbeliever and believer. But as the promise, or the future, was coming upon a nation so was that affecting an individual's life.

Acts 7:23

23 And when he was full forty years old, it came into his heart to visit his brethren the children of Israel.

Abraham's promise of the future was now affecting Moses' life! What so many are sensing in this hour is the fullness of past promise, fullness of past revelation, fullness of the future pressing in. Some react and run. Some deny. A few embrace. You see it has to be in our heart before it is manifested in the earth. The problem is we try to act out a promise, before it is firmly in our heart. Right now what has been promised is bearing down upon the age we are living in.

Acts 7:30

30 And when forty years were expired, there appeared to him in the wilderness of mount Sinai an angel of the Lord in a flame of fire in a bush.

It was not just fire that appeared to Moses but also the future. What Moses saw in the burning bush was a type of his future. He would be one that would be known for the fire of God. What all of us have seen is only a type of our future coming to us. The true future that awaits us is greater than even the shadows of what we've seen. The problem is we lose heart waiting for the future to manifest itself or for the revelation to fully come. I, myself, wrestle with this constantly knowing the revelation that God has given us, and yet not seeing it fully manifest. The only thing that keeps me going is that I know within my heart the revelation is resting. Habakkuk tells us to write the vision down that others when they read it may be able to run with it. Today God writes the revelation of the future upon our hearts and asks us to run with it.

Sometimes the future tarries because we are not yet ready to receive it. Sometimes it tarries because we do not believe God wants to give it to us. But every promise, every revelation, every vision, every dream, will surely come to pass. The revelation or future for

87

your life itself is held in the revelatory realm tarrying for your faith to make it manifest.

Revelation concerning the Plan of God

Ezra 1: 1-3

Let's look at Ezra. Ezra came on the scene to be a king over the nation. He found the scroll of Isaiah and began reading. Imagine his response when he saw his name written by a prophet 150 years before his birth! God's plan, future revelation of this man's life was written in a scroll to be released at a later time. Ezra was an ungodly man converted in one night when he found out his future was already sure! There are coming into the Kingdom those who are having a revelation concerning their future. There is a scroll of your life with your future written upon it. Not only did Ezra have the past written scroll, but also the prophets Jeremiah, Daniel, and Zechariah were alive and prophesying his future as well. I believe many of us today have prophetic words given in the moment of our life upon the earth. But I also believe prophets of past have spoken concerning us as well. We just have not come across the scroll yet!

Now, to come to the Revelation God gave me

concerning what clouds our future so many times. At times, all believers have an encounter where God reveals our future to us, or gives us a revelation, or we see ourselves in a vision doing some great exploit. When these things come, we see and experience them in their purest form. They are in the spirit realm held by the hand of God. When the revelation or the vision starts to manifest upon the earth, it enters into a realm that has sin within it. Sin begins to taint what we saw as pure and it does not look like how we first saw it. We can even begin to think this is not from God. We look at others and blame them that our vision for our life or ministry is not what it should be. At the point of the revelation entering the earth realm, is the point the enemy begins to try to steal or destroy our future concerning what we know we are to do. I have seen so many be caught in this trap as the enemy whispers in their ears and he backs it up by tainting what God first showed us as pure. This is the point leaders lose heart in ministry and give up or quit all together. Many abandon the plan because it is not what they wanted it to look like. But what separates those who will fulfill from those who only see is what Moses experienced. Getting the vision in its pure form in our heart first and then seeing it manifest as it should be. We see a great example of this with Nehemiah as he approached the rebuilding of the walls.

In the season that we are now in, the revelation of God is beginning to manifest in the earth again. What we have all seen in its purest form is already taking root in our hearts. God spoke to me and said do not worry about those who do not participate, like Israel leaving Egypt, all will participate before it is done. Right now God is looking for those who have the revelation of their future firmly fixed in their heart. He wants them to begin to manifest that revelation in the earth realm so the future of others can be unlocked. Do not let the enemy whisper lies in your ear. Do not be discouraged when your future begins to manifest that it does not quite look like you first saw. If we do not lose heart, God's power working through us will bring our future and a perfect clarity in this hour.

Chapter 13

Will Your Life be a Seed for the Harvest?

John 12:24 ... except a corn of wheat fall into the ground and die, it abideth alone: but if it die, it bringeth forth much fruit

God requires those of great calling to not only die to self but may at some time, call upon them to give their very lives for the cause of Christ. Most of us do not think in these terms because of the freedom and liberty we have in this nation. Right now a large number of our brothers and sisters are in nations where their lives can be put in harm's way for their faith. Listen to this most amazing statistic. More than 70 million Christians have been martyred for their faith since 33 AD. This year an estimated 160,000 believers will die at the hands of their oppressors and over 200 million will be persecuted, arrested, tortured, beaten or jailed. In many nations, it is illegal to own a Bible, share your faith, change your faith or allow children under 18 to attend a religious service.

We need to realize we are not exempt because of our national freedom. We already are seeing the beginning stages of intolerance towards Christians and the morality they represent. But are we so busy "doing the work" not of ministry but of self-created monstrosities, that we do not realize what is happening around us? All our good programs will never prepare us for true persecution. Only by being willing seeds will we see the true harvest!

Acts 6:1-7 And in those days, when the number of the disciples was multiplied, there arose a murmuring of the Grecians against the Hebrews, because their widows were neglected in the daily ministration. 2 Then the twelve called the multitude of the disciples unto them, and said, It is not reason that we should leave the word of God, and serve tables . 3 Wherefore, brethren, look ye out among you seven men of honest report, full of the Holy Ghost and wisdom, whom we may appoint over this business. 4 But we will give ourselves continually to prayer, and to the ministry of the word . 5 And the saying pleased the whole multitude: and they chose Stephen, a man full of faith and of the Holy Ghost, and Philip, and Prochorus, and Nicanor, and Timon, and Parmenas, and Nicolas a proselyte of Antioch : 6

Whom they set before the apostles: and when they had prayed, they laid their hands on them . [7] And the word of God increased; and the number of the disciples multiplied in Jerusalem greatly; and a great company of the priests were obedient to the faith.

We all know this passage and have had it preached to us, especially in times of menial tasks needing done and no one participating. We have looked at this scripture as a solution by ministers to avoid doing physical work and lost track of the true meaning. The Grecians were murmuring against the Hebrews because their widows were neglected in the daily ministration. The Word of God had stopped growing. The Church was coming to a transition point. Would they go forward or remain in the same place? This transition was not about helps ministry, serving, or even waiting tables. It was a transition point of putting in place seed for the harvest and fulfilling the original mandate Jesus had given in *Acts 1:8*. As we know, seven Grecian men were selected to serve tables. This was the first transition in the book of Acts of transfer of power and authority to those looked upon as God fearing but not true believers. It was a type and shadow pointing to the Gospel

93

coming to the Gentiles. Seven men selected to be seed for the harvest but only one would be chosen.

The problem at hand was not physical, tables and hungry people, it was spiritual, the Word of God was not increasing. Does this mean no one was preaching the Gospel, or teaching? No, they had the physical problem because of those things. No, the word of God was not some teaching session, it was Jesus Himself, the Living Word abiding within. People's personal relationships with Him were lacking. He was being crowded out by daily chores put upon those leading.

The Apostles had the same problem as anyone doing ministry experiences if they have the Spirit of God moving. The corporate Body or physical structure was overtaking the spiritual relationship. We have experienced this many times in our ministry. To those locally, it appears we may not be growing, however our ministry is not local but more regional, national, and international. As an equipping center or resource center, the number of people locally in a small community may not desire what is offered. But when we start looking at those scattered outside of the area then the numbers go quickly to the thousands. Each time the demand is put upon us, we have to restructure not to maintain or fix a pressing issue, but so we have the time to maintain our spiritual walks.

The LEADERS had determined that they would prioritize their lives and would focus their lives on their relationship with Christ and ministry to him. They basically took the problem, told the people they needed to handle it, and modeled how to get things in order in their walk. The Apostles did not dictate what happened but created opportunity for potential to be released. That is what true apostles have a God given ability to do. The whole multitude made the decision who was to be chosen.

When we get this perspective right, the amount of growth we can experience is unlimited. You see they had no teaching materials, no Bible. Personal growth was not dependent upon hearing messages or reading some book, but was put upon each person to work out their own salvation with fear and trembling. The people themselves were the Bible and Jesus within them was the Living Word. A better way of putting it was when Jesus increased within them, then a multiplication came of disciples, not just

95

converts. In other words when the Living Word, Jesus resident within them, was allowed to increase in ALL of them, not just the leaders, then they had the solution to the problem at hand, true disciples. Even priests believed. As I have researched this, it is believed the number of priests who believed was over 8,000. Now that is influence! That is harvest! That is nothing in comparison to what is coming because the seed has not yet died for the harvest. It now is only being prepared for planting.

As we see this picture, we actually see three types of groups of people represented positionally in walk and function: Outer Court, Inner Court and Holy of Holies. The outer court is a generation of unbelievers who are in great need physically but have not the Living Word abiding within them. They depend solely upon the faith of others. Even today how many are unconsciously doing this with those who are in the Church? We get several calls a week asking to pay utility bills, food, etc.

The second group is in the Holy place, ministering to needs, but not yet fully engaged in ministry to the Lord. This is where many are today and especially the next generation. The desire for service is in place but distraction abounds all around.

It is performing out of duty and to please others than to serve out of relationship and because we love God and understand His ways. Most ministers today are letting needs dictate direction of ministry instead of God directing ministry and needs being met along the way. In the Holy of Holies, is the last group -the advancers or conquerors. They are the ones who have to first conquer the fear of not meeting the needs and making sure their lives are prioritized correctly. This group is the smallest in the Church today. This is where the Jacobs are to be in this hour. Holding the portal of heaven open until Josephs are seasoned enough. The needs are met because of the anointing on their lives and not the strength of youth.

Selfishness is the main problem today. What the Church is fighting the most is not the devil, not the world, not government, or even faith. The main problem everything upon the earth is affected with is the Church itself. If the Church was in the right place, most of these things would be resolved or in process of being resolved. Reformation will sweep the Church once it gets rid of its selfishness. The Church has lost track of the mandate upon it. It is not programs, not conferences, not 24/7 prayer or books and tapes. It is preaching the Kingdom of Christ. We must get back to the Word of God being formed inside of us, the true Living Word of God, not men's opinions. This is the only solution to every single problem we are experiencing. There has to be an awakening, yes to the Word of God, but more so to the already "Living Word of God" inside the already existing Church. You see, as Stephen died and his blood spilled upon the earth, He, along with the "Word of God, Jesus the Living Word" was also planted once again into the earth. This is what brings great harvest. It is all based on someone being a seed, like Jesus, and planting their lives into the earth.

Once we stop having a task mentality with the things of God and look upon even "waiting tables" as a spiritual service unto God, we then will begin the transition into the harvest. The early Church looked at everything as eternal and that they were already living in the eternal realm. For them to wait tables, minister to God or give their lives all had eternal purposes within it. The embrace of the eternal purposes of God for their lives allowed them to do service in menial tasks. We have not taught people this principle yet, as most do not even realize what the eternal purposes are. This moves us from being servants to being friends. Friends have special privilege and are shown honor. When we realize it is an honor to work in menial tasks for the Lord, we will then know the Church is in transition into eternal purposes. Knowing this eternal purpose is what allowed Stephen to give his life so freely. His death was not a transition into eternity but only a greater fulfillment of the life and the "Word of God" abiding within him to manifest eternity present in a greater way. Read the story in *Acts 7*. Stephen did not go up into eternity until he first brought eternity down into the earth. Once the transition was accomplished, the Church was moved into the miraculous. Great growth and great signs and wonders. A greater grace or sphere of influence occurred.

John 12:24... except a corn of wheat fall into the ground and die, it abideth alone: but if it die, it bringeth forth much fruit.

As we consider the life of Stephen, we soon realize a man who has been nameless and faceless suddenly arises to recognition but the recognition holds imprisonment and even death. Like a typical seed planted in a great field, no one seems concerned for the one. No one except the Lord. As Stephen is about to be killed, he brings eternity into the present before he escapes the present and enters eternity. We see his death not only caused a great stir in the earth but also moved heaven. Let's look at five simple points concerning being seed for the harvest.

1. **The City takers – the revolution begins based on the sacrificial living and giving of lives.**

We must realize that every reformation/change comes from a price paid – death. In *Acts 1 – 7*, The Church is advancing by outside forces. In *Acts.7:54-60*, we have the martyrdom of Stephen. This is a transitional point of the Church. Now the Church is advancing because of the forces of heaven. The Church cannot allow heaven to dictate if we continue to empower our circumstances to prevail over us. Someone has to die to the status quo and yield to a higher calling. This requires action over thinking, faith over understanding. Enoch laid his life down to be taken. Joseph laid his life down to be given. Daniel to be poured out, and Isaiah to be challenged.

Acts 7:56 Behold, I see the heavens opened, and the Son of man standing on the right hand of God.

We see a tremendous outcome of Stephen's death. It does not occur upon the earth but in the heavens. Jesus, the Son of God, stood when Stephen was killed. Imagine that, the death of a saint causes the Son of God to rise and take notice. But also all of heaven is in motion, if Jesus stands, everyone stands. I imagine the angels were peering upon Jesus with great expectation concerning the new orders He was about to release upon them! This step is best summed up by saying we need sacrifice instead of selfishness. Stephen's death released the same power that raised Christ from the dead and brought great life into the Church. It brought heaven from a place of resting to a place of attention!

2. **We must discover the power to prevail over every obstacle.**

We cannot reform what still holds power or a grip over us! Where have you positioned yourself? Are you in a place of need or are you ministering to needs and advancing The Kingdom? Just like Stephen, death no longer held a grip upon him. It does not even say he felt pain. God has called us to not just get by with a few simple victories, but to be overcomers in all things. If demons must give way to us, then surely what controls men's hearts will as well! We cannot be living in need all the time but must come to a point of growing up and ministering to the needs of others. This will allow leaders to stop babysitting us and begin to release the advance of heaven. What is bigger in you? Your need or Christ the Hope of Glory? When we give God our lives, we then allow Him to place miracles inside of us. The miracles inside those chosen to wait tables were not for themselves but for those who did not yet believe. *Acts 19:11-12* Paul received, but the people ministered in the miracles! Leaders are to be bringing the power down and the people taking the power out!

3. We must be carriers of the flame of God to ignite the fire that spreads.

The flame of God inside us is to be a supernatural fire coming forth. We must be carriers of influence in society. Stephen's life laid down touched the heart of the people and Paul's heart. The entire Church was scattered abroad, not just the 12 apostles but THE CHURCH! Every person was equipped according to *Eph. 4:11-14. Eph 4:14* Perfect the Saints – outer court. *Eph 4:15* Work of the ministry – Holy Place. *Eph 4:16* Edify the Body – Most Holy Place. This is The Word dwelling inside of us! *Acts 8:8 And there was great joy in that city.* Stephen's death unlocked joy for an entire city, a region was impacted. His death brought reformation to the Church and put them into motion to finally fulfill Jesus' mandate of *Acts 1:8* upon them. It brought not only harvest at Jerusalem but now it would unlock the harvest of the rest of the world!

4. We must have an accurate message of the Spirit and not the message of men.

Truth does not entertain but confronts, convicts, brings change, power, releases destiny, releases cause and purpose. The Gospel is abrasive, it was never meant to be pleasing to our flesh. Stephens's message was not his opinion but was the truth. He spoke concerning the actual actions of those who stood before him confronting the contradictions of their lives. The power we all desire to see comes

103

when the true message of the Kingdom is preached. Truth is more than a technique or four steps to whatever. Truth stands alone and needs no private interpretation. Inside the Church is the message of the Kingdom. It has just become muddy from all the input of what we think it means. The message in the Church is also the very thing to release its destiny. The early Church did not have a Bible, they <u>were</u> the Bible. The true Living Word of God was alive inside of them. Their lives were closely being watched by the world. Their close relationship with the Lord directly influenced the people around them. The Bible will be alive to you when you let Christ be alive inside of you. ***Gal. 1:16 To reveal his Son in me that I might preach him among the heathen; immediately I conferred not with flesh and blood:*** Paul says the message inside of him was because Christ was alive inside of Him! We need to get a revelation of that. Another way of putting it is the message inside of you is the Person living inside of you! The message we are carrying is a message to change the seasons of people's lives and even the earth. The early Church was the final word concerning the issue. Why? Because it was the Word, JESUS!

5. To carry a reformation, we must reach strategic people's hearts in society.

Phillip left waiting tables and went into Samaria and reached Simon who practiced sorcery. The death of Stephen enabled the Church to reach key leaders influencing society in other regions. Now this is reformation. Even Paul was standing and witnessing Stephens's death with approval. But it does not say He participated in the death. I find that interesting. Even in a state of sin, God was holding Paul from a future regret. Stephen's life had to have an influence upon Paul. I believe deep in Paul's heart, who knew what Stephen had just declared was the truth of the matter; was confronted in his death with what he was doing. It only took time to work out the truth Stephen declared to bring change to Paul. After Paul's conversion, he also went into cities and found strategic people to confront with The Kingdom. This is a Biblical pattern of reformation.

Today we focus so much on the poor, and there is nothing wrong with helping them. Jesus said we would have them with us always. The problem is we get so focused on them and do not reach the key people of influence who can make ministry to the poor easier. Because of this one sided focus of the poor, past moves of God have died out. We must ask God who the key people are that we are to reach in society so the reformation can continue.

 The question comes to this. Am I willing to die to selfishness and allow the True Living Word of God to live inside of me? Not what men have told me and I have memorized in my head, but Jesus alive in me! Will I be seed for the harvest? Every time we see a person who has died and lays a portion of their life down, we also see the planting of a portion of the Son of God again into the earth. Imagine if we would die fully and be fully planted as the Church, the words of Jesus would then be fulfilled "…. Greater works than these shall you do…."

ABOUT THE AUTHOR

Greg Crawford has been active in ministry for over 30 years serving in almost every type of leadership role. He is the founder of Jubilee International Ministries which recently relocated to Des Moines, Iowa. He and his wife, Julie, have also co-labored in founding Jubilee School of Ministry and Jubilee International School of Ministry which now has 40+ schools in developing nations. The International School network graduates roughly 5,000 students yearly. They have grown the network of schools to stand on their own within their nation without ongoing support from the United States. Jubilee School of Ministry in the USA has international graduates who have established schools and works in many nations of the world as well. Many have planted churches orphanages, and are involved in high places of influence in governments. Today Jubilee School of Ministry is no longer a class room but is an online school of ministry training with over 350 hours of online instruction.

Apostle Crawford or APG as he is know by, has traveled on numerous international trips, leading teams into nations conducting leadership conferences. He has worked in Cote D Vire,

Nigeria, South Africa, Zambia, and Indonesia. Many of the nations have had reoccurring trips as he has taken teams of ministers with him. He laid the ground work for the apostolic reformation in Nigeria with close to 12 trips to this nation alone, teaching thousands of leaders on team ministry and the apostolic for the first time. With close to 50 ministers ordained under them in the United States, they also provide counsel and insight, helping many church leaders today.

Apostle Crawford has become a spiritual father to many and has a desire to see the generations running together as one voice. He has labored to see the Kingdom expression of reformation and awakening come by travels in Iowa and the United States to help bring this into existence. He is best known for his revelatory teaching style and has a unique and powerful ministry of laying on of hands for impartation. He carries a deep message that release the breath of God to confront the hearts of believers. This has opened the door for him to speak at many national conferences. The revelatory dynamic has enabled him to write over 10 books, write close to 300 hours of classes, some taught by secular colleges, and to send out a bi-monthly teaching through email. His teachings can be found on many websites and have been the lead feature article on Identity Network a leading prophetic voice in America with a web base following of close to 350,000.

He holds a PHD of Ministry which he received Magna Suma Cum Laude. He is ordained with Jim Hodges' Federation of Ministries and Churches International and is in relationship with several well know national voices. Currently he is overseeing The BASE, a ministry located in Des Moines to bring awakening and reformation to the church and culture. The forerunner ministry of the BASE has creative spontaneous worship created in the moment, gift and call devolvement, investment by spiritual fathering, and revelatory instruction with opportunity. More information can be found at the ministry website **www.thebaseiowa.org**

Greg Crawford

Greg Crawford